From FRUSTRATION to FUNNY in 10 Seconds Flat!

3 Steps That Work Every Time You Actually Do Them

Vicki Hannah Lein, MS Counseling

*"Although the world is full
of suffering, it is full also of
the overcoming of it."*

~ Helen Keller, blind & deaf educator

*"If you could see what I see,
you could set yourself free."*

~ Vicki

*"Vicki is funny and wise and I
value her friendship dearly."*

~ Oprah
(if she had ever met Vicki)

A Funny Book About a Serious Topic

Note: You can learn how to move from frustration to funny in 10 seconds flat by going to India and living in a cave for three months, eating only yogurt and seeds

Or

You can rollup your sleeves, sharpen your funny bone, and learn how to stop frustrating yourself and have fun -- most of the time.

Here is the main point of this book:

Life does not frustrate us. We frustrate ourselves by telling ourselves a story that invites us to feel victimized. We tell ourselves we are entitled to have whatever we want when we want it--a story guaranteed to make us miserable and insufferable.

Wow! Talk about starting a book off by heaving a bucket of ice water right straight at the reader's face! Well, yes. Wake up! You are giving your precious joy, energy, and optimism away to strangers who change lanes without signaling or toasters that burn your cinnamon raisin bagel. You have a bad habit of frustrating yourself and now, in three steps that work every time you actually do them, you can reclaim your bouncy spirit and tremendous sense of humor.

When we practice frustrating ourselves, we raise our blood pressure, lower our immune system's ability to fight off disease, and disturb our peace of mind. We also disturb the peace of mind of those innocent people around us, such as those replicas of our DNA who are held captive in our car.

You can learn to stop frustrating yourself and start learning to find the Cosmic Joke more quickly than you can imagine. You are not being captured by Frustration and being hauled off to the Slough of Self-Righteousness. You are leaving The Land of Perspective and Funny and hurling yourself off a cliff.

Stop it. Stop it right now. Learn to stop frustrating yourself and find the funny in 10 seconds flat starting right now. You will live longer and the people around you will be happy you are living longer because you are so much more fun to be around.

Why Listen to Me?

When I lost my central vision 20 years ago, while I was in the middle of a divorce and losing my job, I had to get very good, very fast, at finding the funny. Every day I had the choice of focusing on what was missing in my life or what I had left of my life. I chose to focus on what I had left, and that, my friends, has made all the difference.

I had to get used to asking for help and receiving it graciously, waiting for rides patiently, and finding the humor in situations that begged me to fall on the floor sobbing. Actually, after asking for help and not getting any, my backup plan is to fall on the floor sobbing. I've never had to do this, but it is comforting to have a backup plan.

As a result of losing my central vision, I am kinder, more patient, more grateful, and much, much funnier. Ask anyone who knew me when I could see. I occasionally regress to my old "I want what I want and I want it right now, dammit!" self, but that happens rarely and I catch on quickly and get myself back to the truth: I am one of the luckiest people on the planet. I live surrounded by beauty and love and I've worked very hard to become the kind of person who can see that. There are many ways to be blind.

You don't have to go blind to learn how to find the funny faster, but it helps.

Just kidding. If hardship always resulted in compassion, war would end immediately, and greed would be a word dropped from the dictionary.

For our lives to be full of serenity and joy and laughter and gratitude, we need to take each situation by the horns, as it were, and wrestle it into humorous submission. "Take that! Murphy." (You of the 'what-can-go-wrong-will-go-wrong' religion.) I befriend you! I smile in your general direction!

4

Make yourself this promise and
change your life forever:

I will not sacrifice my joy on the alter
of 'I did not get what I wanted.' I will
not impose my bad mood on other people
because I feel I'm entitled to anything.

Hint: Make friends with Murphy and then when
he strikes, you will find it funny instead of
irritating, unfair, terrible, horrible, or very bad.

If I, a blind, AARP
member, can do it,
you can do it.

This book is for you if:

☺ You are in jail because you gave into your road rage and punched that jerk driver in the nose. Your incarceration has caused you to think that perhaps there is a better way...

☺ You are sick and tired of being frustrated and you are willing to entertain the idea that perhaps you are frustrating yourself.

☺ You did something really stupid or dangerous in a moment of frustrating yourself, such as kicking a dog and falling down the stairs (I did this once) and you don't want the Universe to up the ante and break your leg to get your attention.

☺ You have high blood pressure and your doctor or your friends are telling you to lighten up.

☺ You think you have a great sense of humor, but no one else agrees.

☺ You have a great sense of humor, but somehow you aren't able to find your funny bone when you need it most.

In order to help you find your compassion, remember what the Dali Lama says:

"Be Kind whenever possible. It is always possible."

Frustration Prevention

An ounce of prevention, as they say, is worth a pound of cure. If you can commit to the following **three habits,** you will eliminate almost all of your frustration.

Here are three habits I practice on a daily basis that keep my brain working, get the best out of everyone I encounter, and increase my life expectancy:

Habit #1: **Make Their Day**

Habit #2: **Create a Back Story that Makes You Laugh or Fills You with Compassion**

Habit #3: **Make Friends with Murphy**

Habit #1: Make Their Day

This is one of the rules of improvisation, see Tina Fay's book *Bossypants*, that helps make the world go around more cheerily: **make the other person look good.**

What if, all day long, your goal were to <u>make the day</u> of that clerk in the grocery store, the gas station attendant, or even the teller in the bank? These people will laugh or smile at the smallest provocation. They are happy for a friendly, human connection. As a result of practicing this habit, I've had bank tellers ask if they could follow me around all day.

"Sure," I say, "but following me around all day doesn't pay well -- in monetary terms, anyway."

Here is what Making Their Day looks like:

- **Smile**. Research shows that smiling changes your brain chemistry. When you smile your brain is too stupid to know if you are really happy or not. It starts kicking in those delicious mood altering chemicals. Yum.

Not only that, smiling changes the atmosphere for everyone around you. It's free and it takes fewer muscles to smile than frown, right?

- **Comment on something they are doing well.** "I wish I could pack a bag that quickly," you might say to the guy at Trader Joe's who is cheerfully stuffing your sack with goodies. Ever notice how friendly and helpful the staff is at Trader Joe's? I think their job is to make YOUR day. Make their day right back at them. You'll show them, by golly, who is the Queen of Making Their Day!!

- **Make some kind of joke about something, anything.** Clerks are an easy laugh. Almost everyone is an easy laugh except custom agents. I do not chitchat with them, but I do smile. If you do not have a good sense of humor yet, keep smiling.

- **Say something complimentary and true:** "You make the best chocolate croissants in town. I feel as if I'm back in France."

That's enough for now. Give it a try. You will change your body chemistry.

Habit #2: Create a Back Story that Makes You Laugh or Fills You with Compassion

 Inventing a back story or a reason for the behavior that is inviting you to frustrate yourself, will help prevent Alzheimer's and might make you laugh. You have been practicing for perhaps decades telling yourself a story where the other person is a jerk, so it may take you awhile to shift.

Fear not! **Whatever you practice you get good at, and you are always practicing something.** Start practicing finding the funny or a story that touches your heart and you will become an expert. You will be a kinder person as a result. I promise.

Sample Back Stories

1. Her feet hurt. That is why she is so crabby or slow or careless.

2. He is driving fast and recklessly because he is rushing his children to the hospital

because the barbecue fell on them and the skin is sloughing off his children as he risks life, possibly your life, and limb to get them to the hospital.

This really happened to one of my students. Could you possibly stay mad at someone if you knew this is why they were driving so crazily? If so, this book will not help you.

3. Today is their first day on the job. They have been looking for a job for over a year and they are so excited they can't think straight. Ever been nervous the first time on the job? Cut them some slack.

Habit #3: Make Friends with Murphy

You know Murphy, the guy in charge of making anything that can go wrong, go wrong. He likes to work in three's. If you have a flat tire when you go out to start your car in the morning, for example, you will have a dead cell phone when you try to call AAA. Then, as you throw a little temper tantrum and kick the car, you break your toe.

Murphy is not picking on you, and it's best not to pick a fight with Murphy. Murphy will always win. Always. The sooner you surrender with a smile on your face, the sooner your life will start getting better.

When you notice he is messing with you, smile and say to yourself, "Welcome, old friend. I know you. You are my buddy. I am not going to spend any time yelling at you about my fate. I accept that it is just my turn for a Murphy Day. I can handle it. Bring it on."

I promise you, this will help. It certainly won't hurt you while your temper tantrum might. Yelling at the waitress, car mechanic, receptionist, bank clerk will add icky energy, raise your blood pressure, and invite the people around you to behave badly.

Use your Murphy Day as an extra challenge to Make Their Day. You will not let Murphy ruin your day AND an innocent or not so innocent bystander's day. You simply will not let Murphy win. Murphy is your friend. Murphy is your friend. Say it with me: "Murphy is my friend."

This habit works anytime you actually do it. Congratulate yourself on your self-discipline and your amazing sense of humor and perspective.

I will weave these three habits through the rest of the book. You need to hear them seven times to learn them. I'm not promising you will hear each habit seven times. You can always reread the book if necessary. Or you can teach this material to a friend or partner. I'm teaching you to fish, not giving you fish. Get your worms ready!

The 3 Magic Steps That Work Every Time You Actually Do Them

To coin a phrase, this is not rocket science. This strategy is simple, but only you can do it. You have to be ready to change, just like that proverbial lightbulb, and you have to commit to practicing behaving differently.

Until now you have practiced for many years frustrating yourself. You've been telling yourself that those irritating events and people frustrate you, but actually, you are very good at frustrating yourself. It's a big step to admit that. If you can't admit that, you just wasted $2.99. Want to write me a nasty letter of complaint? That would show me, by golly! How dare I suggest that you have the power to frustrate yourself or find the joke! Oh, that is the title of the book, after all, so get over yourself and prepare to learn a new habit.

Get ready for some great news: it only takes 26 days to change a habit. If you commit yourself to these three steps for 26 days, you will succeed in drastically reducing the time you spend frustrating yourself. I promise!

Challenge: If you come upon a situation which you think is impossible for anyone to experience without frustration, email me at vickihannahlein@ gmail.com with the subject line: Unfrustrate me!

I dare you! I will give it my best shot.

Are you ready? Here we go!

STEP 1: Catch Yourself Frustrating Yourself

No event frustrates you. No person frustrates you. You frustrate yourself by telling yourself a powerful story you believe to be true. "What is happening to me right now would frustrate anyone and there is no other way I could possibly respond to this event!"

Telling yourself this story guarantees that you will succeed in frustrating yourself because anyone and everyone who tells themselves this story will feel frustration. This story supplies instant gratification. If you tell yourself how unfair it is, and get yourself all riled up, your body will produce a yummy drug: adrenaline. You can get addicted to your own adrenaline as surely as any other mood-altering drug.

Frustration is a mild form of rage. That's one reason it is so dangerous to practice frustrating yourself. Frustration opens the spigot to your rage. The feeling of rage floods your brain, making it difficult to find your reason.

No one is at the mercy of their rage. If you practice rage, you will become addicted to it. Anger management is all about getting in the way of this physical addiction caused by a thought, a story. "I can't help it" is a lie.

Want proof? Let's say someone who was raised by a ragaholic becomes a ragaholic. Not surprising. Let's say this person is practicing their rage addiction because someone tipped over a paint can and bright red paint is now all over the patio next to the pool.

Let's assume the person raging notices little footprints in the paint that head directly to the pool. Let's assume the raging person looks in the pool and sees their beloved two-year-old daughter floating face down in the clear blue water.

Let's assume the child does not have gills and needs air instead of water to breathe.

Do you think the rage will disappear instantly as the parent dives in the pool to save her daughter? Or do you think this mother will start yelling at the little girl floating face down, tiny bubbles bursting above her submerged face? Will she put her hands on her hips and say: ""How many times have I told you..."

Of course the rage will be gone instantly because the story of "My Rights have Been Violated!" has just been replaced with the story "I'd better do something quickly or my child will die."

I'm telling you this dramatic story to prove a point: we can ALWAYS get ourselves out of a frustration/rage attack. Always.

Catching yourself might save your life or the life of someone else. That is not funny but it is true.

Step 1: Requires you to catch the story.

The sooner you catch it the better, but you can't change frustration to funny until you realize you, once again, aren't you adorable, have told yourself the Frustration Story.

Now that you've caught your frustration story, you must release it.

STEP 2: Release the Story and the Tension You've Created

You've caught the story, you have noticed you are clenching your teeth or your fists. Great work. Now you let that story flow right out of your body.

You can do this several ways:

- **Take a breath.** Breathe deeply. Make a sound as you let all that blood pressure rising emotion out of your body. This type of breathing also works in childbirth, fyi.

- **Smile.** You change your brain chemistry when you smile. Really. When you smile you tell your brain you are happy, and your brain is too stupid to know if you are really happy or not, so it starts producing all those yummy mood altering chemicals. Happy day!

I told you this before, but it is worth repeating. Remember, you need to hear something seven times to learn it. Go tell this to five innocent bystanders and you will remember to smile forever. You will also get to practice not caring about what other people think all the time, which will release your creativity and might perhaps save the world. No kidding.

- **Sing** Happy New Day to Me! Or any song that makes you feel good or distracts you from frustrating yourself. Put on the clown nose you have in the passenger seat next to you--do anything to stop the story. You will get very good at this with practice.

- **Sigh.** Sighing also instantly shifts your energy and focus.

- **Yawn.** If you can get yourself to yawn, you can change your life forever. Yawning brings lots of oxygen to your brain, and when you are starting to frustrate yourself, your brain needs all the oxygen it can get.

- **Smile and Raise your hands above your head in a V.** Do it right now and see what happens to you. Your whole body will change. This is a universal sign of joy and triumph. You simply cannot be angry and resentful and smile and raise your arms at the same time. If you try to remain self-righteous you will feel like a fool and that will bring you back to your senses. Win/win.

STEP 3: Rebait your hook to Compassion or Gratitude. Hereafter Called Gratitoot.

You've been hooked on a story that frustrates or angers you. After you catch yourself creating this story and then do something to release the story from your body, it's time to replace your frustrating story with one that amuses you or stimulates your compassion. Finding reasons to be grateful that you have a flat tire on the Golden Gate Bridge will make you smile. You will start to find the situation funny. You will have perspective. Your blood pressure will drop. Your spouse may decide to stay married to you.

Perspective is everything. Believe me, my friend who just spent two weeks in the hospital having seizures, eighteen months after undergoing chemotherapy for her brain cancer, would trade you her cancer for your flat tire in a heartbeat.

Here are some things you can say to yourself to help you rebait the story you've been hooked on that is making you miserable, for one that will lead you to Compassion or Gratitoot:

- **Oh, Well. Maybe Later.** You didn't get what you wanted right when you wanted it. So what? Say "Oh, well. Maybe later." and experience the thrill of being a grown up.

- **Actually, This is a Good Thing.** Making up a reason why it is a good thing that the electricity just went out will keep you plenty busy.

- **Make Their Day.** This is the prevention habit on steroids. Instead of leaking your bad mood on anyone else, rise to the challenge of making someone else's day. How could you make this person who just caused you hours of delay laugh? You can do it!

- **This Time for Sure!** Say this in a Bullwinkle accent, and you will have your brain and sense of humor back instantly.

- **This is Perfect!** For advanced players only: My Friend, *insert your friend or family member's name here*, Would LOVE to Have My Problem Instead of the One She Has. Telling yourself that children are starving usually doesn't work. Our new story needs to be personal to break through our Frustration Habit.

These Rebating the Hook stories don't have to create belly laughs. Our new stories need to help us see how ridiculous we are. We are all ridiculous a lot of the time. So what? Let's remember why angels are able to fly and practice taking ourselves more lightly.

Let's not take ourselves so seriously, shall we? Let's save some of our precious energy for things that matter, such as appreciating the people we love and work with. Let's be grateful for our very good luck. Our car may be stuck in traffic, but we have a car., and streets that don't have giant death holes in them. And what about that amazing cooperation of all the people stuck with you? It's a miracle, it is, and you will live a much more fulfilling life the more you remember to cherish every moment.

Look around. It's not hard, no matter what your circumstances are, to find LOTS of people who have it much harder than you do. Are you legally blind as I am? Then shut up about how unfair your life is.

Introduction to Unfrustrating Yourself Practice

Invitations to Frustrate Yourself

Since I have been practicing this From Frustration to Funny thing for decades, I have lots of examples to help you out. If, however, in the course of reading this book, you think you have come upon the Absolutely Most Frustrating Event of the Century, email me at vicki@findthefunnyfaster.com with the Subject line: Unfrustrate Me! I dare you! And I will give it my best shot.

The next section of this book is full of **Invitations to Frustration**, situations that most people react to with anything from annoyance to getting put in the back seat of a police car for a "small" temper tantrum on the road.

For each invitation to frustrate yourself, I will give you concrete examples of the *3 Steps That Work Every Time You Actually Do Them:*

A. CATCH YOURSELF frustrating yourself.

B. RELEASE THE FRUSTRATION from your body

C. REBAIT YOUR HOOK with a new story of compassion or gratitude. I sometimes call it Reboot to Gratitoot. (Imagine pulling down on a train whistle when you Gratitoot. Gratitoot, toot!)

Let me unpack these three steps a little more:

STEP 1: CATCH YOURSELF

This is the step where you Catch your behavior. I'm going to have fun with this part, mugging for the camera a bit. I'm hoping by exaggerating, we will all start to see the humor in our behavior and take ourselves less seriously.

My goal is to have fun in every stage of this book. I will be amusing myself most of the time. If you enjoy my exaggerations too, well that is gravy.

STEP TWO: RELEASE THE FRUSTRATION from your body

You Release whatever story you are telling yourself that is causing you to feel frustration.

This often involves taking a deep breath and smiling. Both of these behaviors shift your body and brain chemistry. It's magic and it takes only a few seconds to shift.

STEP THREE: REBAIT YOUR HOOK by

telling yourself a new story -- you Reboot.

I will show you how to do this by showing you one way to find the funny in that particular situation. You will create your own ways, and I invite you to share them on my blog at Find the Funny Faster, www.findthefunnyfaster. com. Let's all become experts at laughing more and beating our joy to death, less!

Are you ready to change your life?

Are you ready to have more fun, enjoy getting up in the morning and dazzling your friends and your bedmate?

Okay, then--here we go!

"Set small, achievable goals that can be accomplished quickly and then do them."
~Michael Jordan

Practice Getting from Frustration to Funny in 10 Seconds Flat

Situation 1

You are driving in light traffic, minding your own business, being the great driver you always are, when someone changes lanes in front of you and you have to break to keep from hitting them.

The Old You:

You slam your hand on the steering wheel, and swear at the jerk, that crappy driver in front of you who has no consideration for

anyone except his stupid self. You think about riding his rear bumper and laying on your horn. That would feel so damned good! You get lost in this fantasy for a moment.

A. The New You:
Then you imagine running into the back of his car to teach him a lesson. You think about illegally using your phone to call and report him to the police, risking getting an expensive ticket yourself. Then, as if by magic, **YOU CATCH YOURSELF** frustrating yourself. Consciousness and sanity return.

B. You Release the story you've been telling yourself that has you all in a tizzy. You notice calmly the other driver's mistake, and you take a deep breath and sigh. "Wow!" you tell yourself, "That was close."

C. You Rebait Your Hook with a new story that makes you laugh or creates compassion.

You say out loud, "Boy am I lucky! My reflexes are so lightening quick I was able to save the day. What a fine fellow I am!" You put on your Crown you bought especially to keep in the car because you don't want to get arrested for road rage.

You have successfully Rebaited Your Hook and Rebooted to Gratitoot. You pull on your imaginary train whistle.

Your thinking brain is working again, so you are able to react quickly when you discover the reason the driver pulled into your lane.

The reason: A humongous truck tire has fallen off a flatbed truck. You are able to swerve and miss hitting any other car.

The guy behind you is less fortunate. Because he has not read this amazing book, he is still practicing throwing temper tantrums. He is so full of righteous indignation, he is unable to react fast enough and smashes his brand new Lexus into the truck tire. Another driver slams into him, giving him whiplash.

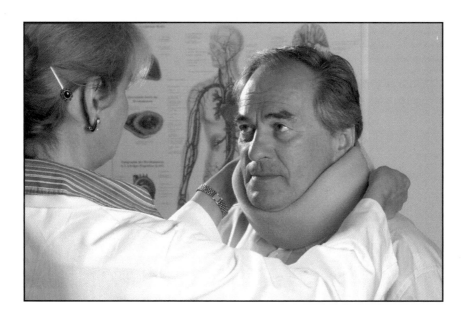

He suffers for the rest of his life with this pain in his neck, never realizing he **is** the pain in his neck and everyone else's.

The ambulance arrives and people are hauled off to the hospital, but not you. You are safely by the side of the road calling your children to tell them how much you love them.

Boy, are you glad you have learned to move from frustration to funny in 10 seconds flat! You vow to recommend this book to everyone you know. You post on Facebook and Twitter from your phone after you call your partner and tell her how much you appreciate her patience with you. She tells you not to worry about getting her a present next Valentine's Day. You bliss out with relief.

Situation 2

You are in a checkout line at a grocery store and a woman in front of you slows things down when she looks for 7 cents in her purse. She digs through one compartment, muttering to herself, and then looks through another section. She has many, many zippered sections in her purse, you notice.

The Old You:
You think to yourself, "What an ignorant jerk! Just give the clerk a dollar, for crying out loud! I have places to go and things to do!" You tap your foot, you clear your throat, and look back to the other customers waiting behind you. You roll your eyes. You clench your fists. You are about ready to say something mean and sarcastic, when, as if by magic,

A. **The new YOU appears and YOU CATCH YOURSELF.**

B. You **Release** the story that has been exasperating you. You take a deep breath and smile. Then you look around and notice headlines that catch your attention. You read the story of the tabloids in the rack and find out that Angelina Jolie is really an alien. You sigh with disappointment.

Sighing also magically helps shift you out of your "I'm entitled to not have to wait" story that has been making you so miserable.

C. **You Rebait Your Hook and Reboot to Gratitoot.** You get interested in the transaction. Just how long can this take? You start rooting for her to find the money. You might even try to make her laugh by saying something like, "You are looking for a 7-cent solution." You are cleverly alluding to a film, the 7-Percent Solution, about that wily addict, Sherlock Holmes. You don't care if anyone listening gets the allusion. You have amused yourself and you are, once again, a hero.

You can't believe how lucky you are to have gotten stuck behind this woman searching for 7 cents. You got a chance to practice shifting from frustration, and, though it took a bit longer than 10 seconds this time, you are getting better every day.

You smile and then notice the white cane with the red tip leaning against the counter. The woman is blind! That is why it took her so long to find those 7 pennies. Whew! You almost insulted a blind woman who took an extra minute to look for change, change which she could not see well. You narrowly escaped being an insensitive jerk.

> ### "Aren't I adorable!"
> Say this to yourself every time
> you make a mistake.

Situation 3

Your new car won't start. You have left your home this morning with just enough time to get to a very important meeting. If you miss this appointment, you might lose the account, your job, the man of your dreams, or the chance to meet Oprah.

The Old You:

You keep turning the key and grinding the engine. You stop and swear. Then you grind the engine again. Then you say to yourself, "I can't believe this! This is a fairly new car. I just had it serviced. I can't be late. I can't be late! I CANNOT be late! Horrible, terrible, unfair consequences will be mine if I am late. Why does this always happen to me?"

A. The New You:

Then, hearing yourself whine -- and not enjoying this unpleasant sound, **YOU CATCH YOURSELF.**

B. You **Release** your self-pitying story. You stop grinding the engine and take a deep breath. You sigh. You shake your hands out in front of you and remember this is a very good thing to do to keep your joints young. This thought makes you smile to yourself.

C. **You Rebait Your Hook** to a story of gratitude. You say to yourself or out loud, "I am so lucky! I needed some time to myself. I've been hurrying and worrying. This is a reminder to not take life so seriously. I have options. I can call a friend or AAA. In fact, it's Nancy's birthday today and I was going to give her a call anyway."

You try to start the car again, and it starts right up because you have been such a good person. You are, quite simply, a hero again.

You call Nancy before you leave your driveway because you do not want to get a ticket for being unsafe and talking on the phone while you are driving. What a good friend you are!

Situation 4

You can't find your keys. You are late for a very important appointment. A small part of you remembers that you had this same situation happen to you recently, but this memory is not enough to stop you from telling yourself a story guaranteed to frustrate you.

The Old You:

You blame someone else or denigrate yourself: "Who the hell took my car keys. I left them right here on the dresser and they are not here, dammit!" "I'm so stupid. I am always losing things. Even my dog doesn't like me anymore." You stomp around your home, slamming drawers. You catch your foot on the leg of a dining room chair, and fall to the floor. You are about ready to amp yourself up into a really delightful explosion, and then,

A. **The New You Appears!** As if by magic, **YOU CATCH YOURSELF.**

B. You **Release** your self-pitying story by saying out loud, "My keys are right where I put them. I'm just sure of that." You smile. Your problem-solving brain starts working again, now that it is not drowned in adrenalin.

C. You Rebait Your Hook with a new story to Gratitoot. You start singing, "Happy missing keys to me! Happy missing keys to me! Happy missing keys, aren't I adorable. Happy missing keys to me!"

Factoid: When we frustrate ourselves, our brains don't work as well and we tend to make more and more mistakes. You know this is true!

When we do something as novel as singing to ourselves, our thinking, problem-solving brain gets to start working for us again. Hallelujah!

Mistake Prevention: Being the imperfectly recovering perfectionist that I am, I try to laugh at my mistakes and then figure out a system so I won't make that same mistake again. Since I am legally blind, I can't scan to find things I've put down without thinking. This has forced me to learn to put my glasses and house keys in the

same place every time. (No, I can't lose my car keys because I have no car keys, because I cannot drive, because I am blind and all.)

Feel a little guilty now for throwing that temper tantrum? Don't. I would love to be able to drive and forget where I put my car keys so I could learn how to find the funny faster and put my car keys in the same place every time.

Situation 5

You wake up and the weather is too cold, too hot, too rainy, too windy, too overcast; in short, not to your liking. Today you are goldilocks and you want the weather to be just right.

The Old You:

You complain about the weather, as you have for decades, to whomever you run into that day . If you can't find anyone to complain to, you complain to yourself, muttering as you brush your teeth.

The weather stubbornly does not change. All day long you look at the weather and mutter. You convince yourself you really do have SAD, Seasonal Affective Disorder, and why not? Bad things are always happening to you. You are lactose intolerant, sensitive to gluten, and you have allergies.

A. The New You Emerges:

The world is simply against you. But because you have been practicing finding the funny, your complaining starts to amuse you. The amusement center of your brain is stimulated. You are having more trouble taking all of your complaining seriously, and **YOU CATCH YOURSELF.**

B. You **Release** your misery-inducing stories. "What an amazing complainer I am!" you say as you smile to yourself. "Complaining about the weather is the worst use of my energy I can think of. I will practice now saying "Yes!" to what is. I am so adorable."

C. **You Rebait Your Hook and Reboot to Gratitoot.** You say out loud or to yourself,"I'm so lucky to be alive today! I love the (wind, rain, overcast, heat, humidity, etc.) because it wakes me up to what a lucky fellow I am! Say it even if you do not believe it. It will work anyway.

> *"Everyone talks about the weather, but no one does anything about it."*
> ~Mark Twain

Situation 6

You are blind. You used the Find tool for two years to help you edit your tome of 500 pages. You could do that because the color you selected to highlight words is dark enough for you to see it. You try using the Find function, and you discover, to your horror, that the highlight which you have no control over now in this one tool, is way too light for you to see it. The Find function is now useless to you. You have not done anything wrong. You do not deserve this. And remember, you are blind and all.

The Old You:

You scream, "This is not helping! This is hurting! Apple is supposed to be so great at making technology accessible for people with disabilities, why have they done this to me? I can't help edit my own books anymore. I am helpless, lost, more disabled because some jerk decided to mess with the highlight function in the Find tool!"

A. The New You Emerges:

You are ready to cry, allowing your self-pity to splash down your face. Then, because you have been working on moving from frustration to funny, **YOU CATCH YOURSELF**.

B.

You **Release** the tension you have put in your body. You stop driving your wellbeing over a cliff. You take a deep breath and smile. For good measure, you lift your arms above your head as you smile and yell, Epic win!"

C.

You Rebait Your Hook and Reboot to Gratitoot. You say, "Well, how about that? Actually, this is a good thing because..." and then you wait for some inspiration. You are smiling while you wait. Finally, it comes to you: "This is actually a good thing because now I won't strain my eyes when I work on this book with my dear friend, Jan. She can read me the sentence and I can edit

44

with my ears instead of my hard-working eyes. I will save my preciously limited eyesight! How lucky I am the highlight color got changed in the Find function."

You do not have to be convinced that this is true. You have amused yourself, and stopped the rampaging train from crashing into the rock wall. Success is yours. Gloat a bit. Smug is better than frustration anytime.

> *"It's not the load that breaks you down. It is the way you carry it."*
> ~Lou Holtz

Situation 7

You are waiting in the car for your partner to join you. You are always on time or early and your partner is always late. Even though they said they were ready to go, you always, always, always are left waiting in the car.

The Old You:

You fume. "He said he was ready, again and he wasn't ready, again, and here I am wasting my time waiting for him, again! Does he think his time is more important than mine? He does! He does not care about me. He is always doing this to me and I've just plain had it!:

A. The New You Emerges:

You prepare what you are going to yell at your partner the moment he opens the door to the garage, blissfully unaware of how wrong he is. His lack of awareness pisses you off even more. You furrow your brow, you purse your lips, and then, as if by magic, **YOU CATCH YOURSELF.**

B. You **Release** your self-righteous story. You realize you are catching yourself, sooner rather than later after all your practice. You take a deep breath and smile. Whew! What a close call. You almost leaked your immaturity and self-righteousness all over your tardy mate. "I'm just like Michael Jordan," you think to yourself and smile. "I know how to set small, achievable goals and then meet them."

C. You Rebait Your Hook and Reboot to Gratitoot. When your beloved partner appears, you say, "I'm so glad you are here and we can get going. And, while I was waiting I thought of a great idea to solve the problem of me waiting in the car for you. Since I don't want you to rush and worry and be afraid I'm going to be all mad at you, I have a brilliant solution. Would you like to hear it now or later?

"You want to hear my brilliant solution now? terrific. From now on when I ask you if you are ready, you say you are ready only if you have everything you need to head to the door: keys, wallet, etc. If you are close to ready but not completely ready, you will tell me you are preready. I will know to keep doing what I'm doing and not head to the car. When you are completely ready, you will tell me you are ready and we will go to the car and have another lovely adventure. Sound good? Yes, I am brilliant. Thank you for noticing."

Situation 8

You get in what appears to be the shortest line in the grocery store. A few carts pull in behind you. You soon discover your clerk is new and is going very slowly. You are stuck because you are boxed in by the carts behind you. You have a very important meeting to get to, and being in this line might make you late.

The Old You:

You start to throw an inner temper tantrum, "Just my luck!" you say, "No matter which checkout line I choose, it is the slowest. Why can't they train their checkers better. Oh, My God! She is calling to check on the price of bananas. Doesn't she know the code by heart? What an idiot!"

A. The New You Emerges:

Why is there no system in place to handle this? She is the slowest, most incompetent checker I have ever seen! I don't deserve this! It's not fair!" Then, as if by magic, you hear your ridiculous, adorable self, and **YOU CATCH YOURSELF.**

B. You **Release** your story of entitlement and judgement. "Wait just a lovely moment," you say to yourself, "This is my precious life here, my only precious life. Do I want to waste one single second getting frustrated? No, I do not." You take a deep breath and smile.

C. **You Rebait Your Hook** and Reboot to Compassion. You then say to yourself, "This is probably this woman's first day on the job. Do I not know what it is like to have trouble learning a new skill? Yes, I do, by golly!"

You suddenly switch from irritation to compassion. You smile at the clerk and you smile at the others waiting. They may think you are crazy, but you do not care. You are free! Free!

You fill a rush of joy and satisfaction. You have finally made friends with Murphy! Success! Yahoo!

From FRUSTRATION to FUNNY in 10 Seconds Flat!

3 Steps That Work Every Time You Actually Do Them

Situation 9

You are feeling smug because you just managed to save yourself from frustration in the previous situation. But, low and behold, Murphy is not through with you yet.

You turn to smile at the woman behind you just in time to see a kid standing in the cart. Suddenly the kid sneezes and does not cover his nose and mouth. You look down and see bits of snot on your new cashmere bright blue sweater. Mucus continues flowing from the boy's nose into his mouth. The boy grins at you.

The Old You:

You say to yourself, "I was so good at not frustrating myself when I got boxed into the slow lane, but this is just too much! My new sweater! Why can't parents leave their snot-nosed children at home? Why bring them to the supermarket? Why can't they teach them to cover their mouths when they sneeze? The world is going to hell in a hand basket!"

A. The New You Emerges:
Then, as if by magic, you see the face
of the bedraggled mother of the snot-
nosed child, and you are brought back to
your senses. **YOU CATCH YOURSELF.**

B. You **Release** your story of being a victim
of merciless fate. You say goodbye to
your belief that this is really too much,
really unfair, and smile at the snot-
nosed boy and his harassed mother.

C. You Rebait Your Hook and Reboot to
compassion. "Want a tissue?" You say to the
mom in a friendly tone. You always carry
a tissue for just such an emergency.

The mom grins sheepishly and says, "Thanks
so much. I would have stayed home with him
because of his cold, but I needed to come to the
pharmacy to get insulin for his older sister who
is in school today. I thought I'd get him some
comfort food while I was here. I'm so sorry he
sneezed on you. Can I give you some money to
pay to dry clean your beautiful sweater?"

You nobly decline her offer.

Your checker is finally ready for you, and you

smile at her and say, "You are really working hard. You don't need to hurry with me. Just take your time."

"Thanks so much," she says, grinning at you. "This is my first day and I'm a little nervous."

"Ah, ha!" you think to yourself. "I was right!" You love being right and that feeling of goodwill stays with you the rest of the day.

You are a little late for the meeting, but it hasn't started. You realize this was another opportunity to practice saying "Yes" to what is and letting go of urgency.

You have Rebooted to Celebration.

You realize, suddenly, that you are getting better and better, faster and faster, at letting go of the frustrating stories you create for yourself. You now know how to replace frustration with gratitude or compassion. You are really glad you did not have to take that three-month trip to India and live in a cave to learn how to find serenity in the midst of chaos.

You are amazing!

Situation 10

It is summer. You live in a rainy climate, such as Oregon, and the weather has finally warmed up. You are so happy because sunny mornings are your favorite thing.

Then you hear the jackhammer in the street right in front of your house. You go outside to check out the situation, and see the sign: Construction Project. Ending date: November.

The Old You:

"November?" you say to yourself, "November? That's four months from now! Four months of construction noises. You've ruined my summer! There is no way I can enjoy my whole summer now because of this stupid construction!"

You go outside and start yelling at the construction workers who ignore you. This just makes you more furious. You pick up a rock, throw it at the guy with the jack hammer. Usually, you can't hit the side of a barn, but today your throw is accuracy itself. You hit the guy on the forehead. He falls over in a pile of helmet and hammers. Men rush to his side. The paramedics are called and pronounce him dead at the scene. The police come and haul you away and you are sentenced to ten years for manslaughter. All your friends and family desert you. Your life is ruined forever.

Just kidding!

A. The New You Was There All the Time:

Your life is not ruined because you did not throw a temper tantrum with a rock. You did not go outside. As soon as you started to frustrate yourself, you caught the signs. You noticed your jaw clenching. You noticed your shallow breathing. As if by magic, **YOU CAUGHT YOURSELF**. You fall on the floor in relief.

B. You have already **Released** the story, **Rebaited** your hook with a new story, and **Rebooted** to Gratitoot at the same time. The steps are melting together as you practice moving from frustration to funny in 10 seconds flat.

C. You continue to **Rebait Your Hook and Reboot to Gratitoot.** You decide the jackhammer sound is perfect. You write a positive rap song, put it on You Tube and it goes viral. Your new career is born. So actually, it was a great thing that the construction project is right in front of your home. (I'm listening to the sound of a jack hammer as I type this. I walk my talk, Baby!)

Situation 11

You are on a conference call with six other people whom you respect. You have all agreed that these weekly conference calls will begin and end on time. These are three-hour calls, so you are grateful they won't go overtime. But, as you approach the three-hour limit, you realize your group call will go overtime.

The Old You:

You start to get angry, "We agreed!" You snarl inwardly. This high-powered group of individuals all agreed we would begin and end on time, and we are going to go over, possibly way over time. I'm exhausted. I can't listen well anymore. I don't want to disappoint anyone. I don't want to be the only person who drops out at the agreed upon time.

A. The New You Emerges:

You could choose to go along to get along and be resentful for days or YOU CATCH YOURSELF. Whew! A near miss.

Hooray for the New You!

B. You **Release** the story of how unfair it is that someone else is not taking care of you and you have to take care of yourself. You smile at your folly and take a deep breath. You have a task: how can you graciously stick to the agreement? You think of the book *The Power of a Positive No* by William Ury. You now get a chance to practice saying no firmly and kindly.

C. You **Rebait Your Hook and Reboot to Gratitoot**. You choose not to break into the conversation, and, instead, type an email to the group members. Subject: "I love you all but I'm cooked." In the body of the email, you explain that your listening is suffering and you will disconnect from the call now. "Talk to you next week" you type cheerfully.

Result: You feel great. You've had to let go of the thought that you might be missing something. This feeling of urgency is familiar and a feeling you have learned to notice and not trust. Instead, you have chosen to trust your body that tells you your pop up timer is out.

You decide you rock! You enjoy the rest of your day, week, and life. You remember who you really are and what your life can be like.

Epilogue

Did you have a good time learning how to follow the three steps that work every time you actually do them? I had a great time writing this little book.

I had so much fun in fact, I am going to continue speaking on this subject in my podcast:

Smart Thoughts for Stupid Moments on iTunes.

Please subscribe and send me challenges. **Unfrustrate this situation;** I dare you! Segments will appear as often as I receive challenges from you.

Bon Voyage!

This is how you'll feel when you learn to find the funny faster.

More Kindle books from Vicki Hannah Lein

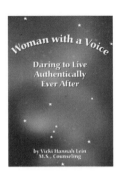

Smart Thought for Stupid Moments

available on lulu.com and amazon.com

Woman with a Voice: Daring to Live Authentically Ever After

available on amazon.com and bookstore.xlibris.com

Cruelty is Not Cool

available on lulu.com and amazon.com

Note: You do not have to own a Kindle to read a Kindle book. You can download a free Kindle Reader app to use on any computer or iPad.

From FRUSTRATION to FUNNY in 10 Seconds Flat!

3 Steps That Work Every Time You Actually Do Them

New **Cruelty is Not Cool** Campaign

Sign up NOW on

crueltyisnotcool.com

to get your free introduction to the book <u>The Radical Kindness Warrior Handbook</u>, as well as songs, and other great stuff to help you **find your best when you are at your worst.**

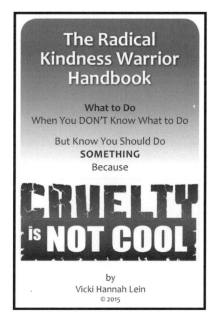

The Radical Kindness Warrior Handbook

What to Do
When You DON'T Know What to Do

But Know You Should Do
SOMETHING
Because

by
Vicki Hannah Lein
© 2015

61

Need a Speaker?

Award-winning international educator, Vicki Hannah Lein, MS Counseling, brings her 30 years of experience as a teacher trainer, therapist , consultant, and international speaker to serve your group. Using humor, original songs, interactive activities, Vicki will customize her talk to deliver your message in a way your members will find unforgettable. Content-rich yet superbly entertaining, Vicki's keynotes will get your gathering off to a rousing start or close with customized songs and sketches to bring your event to an unforgettable close.

Need an educational consultant?

Visit Vicki's Educational site: **Outrageously Alive Education,** **www.outrageouslyalive.com**

Remember to **Find the Funny Faster with Vicki Hannah Lein**

www.findthefunnyfaster.com

Social Media

 Twitter: @vickihannahlein

 Facebook: www.facebook.com/Outrageousvisions

 Facebook: www.facebook.com/stepintoyourgreatness

 Linkedin: www.linkedin.com/pub/vicki-hannah-lein/6/152/757

 Amazon Author Page: www.amazon.com/Vicki-Hannah-Lein/e/B00FCCSFMG/ref=sr_ntt_srch_lnk_4?qid=1381953631&sr=8-4

Books and E books available at:

Lulu.com

Bookstore.Xlibris.com

Amazon.com